THE LITTLE BOOK OF
LEBRON JAMES

The right of David Clayton to be identified as the Author of the Work has been
asserted by him in accordance with the Copyright, Designs and Patents Act 1988.

First published in 2024 by OH
An Imprint of HEADLINE PUBLISHING GROUP

2 4 6 8 10 9 7 5 3 1

Disclaimer:

Cataloguing in Publication Data is available from the British Library

ISBN 978-1-80069-631-0

Compiled and written by: David Clayton
Editorial: Victoria Denne
Designed and typeset in Avenir by: Andy Jones
Project manager: Russell Porter
Production: Rachel Burgess
Printed and bound in China

Headline's policy is to use papers that are natural,
renewable and recyclable products and made from
wood grown in well-managed forests and other
controlled sources. The logging and manufacturing
processes are expected to conform to the
environmental regulations of the country of origin.

HEADLINE PUBLISHING GROUP
An Hachette UK Company
Carmelite House, 50 Victoria Embankment, London EC4Y 0DZ

www.headline.co.uk   www.hachette.co.uk

THE LITTLE BOOK OF
LEBRON JAMES

IN HIS OWN WORDS

CONTENTS

INTRODUCTION

Over a career spanning more than two decades, LeBron James has cemented himself as one of the greatest basketball players of all time – if not the greatest. Whether you consider him the GOAT or not, his impact on the sport is indisputable, and he's not finished yet.

A career defined by difficult decisions, it could have all played out very differently. What if he'd chosen American football instead of basketball? What if he'd stayed with the Cleveland Cavaliers for his whole career? What if he'd never joined the LA Lakers? This turbulent journey has made LeBron's career as fascinating to follow as it has been successful. And it wasn't an easy start, either. Raised by his mother in Akron, Ohio, LeBron's escape route from "the projects" was sport – and although he could have had a career in American football, he chose basketball as his pathway to fame and fortune.

Recognized in high school as a future superstar, he was dubbed "The Chosen One" at the mere age of 17, and in 2003 he was selected as the Cleveland Cavaliers' first pick at the NBA draft. In his first season, he was voted Rookie of the Year and remained with his home city team until 2010.

His controversial decision to join the Miami Heat paid off, winning back-to-back NBA championships in 2012 and 2013, but he returned to the Cleveland Cavaliers in 2014 to fulfill his promise of helping them win the championship, delivering their first ever championship victory in 2016.

After a few more years with the Cleveland Cavaliers, LeBron left once more, this time to join the LA Lakers and win his fourth championship in 2020. While there in 2023, he replaced Kareem Abdul-Jabbar as the NBA's record points scorer.

From a potential American football prodigy to a bona fide basketball sensation, movie star, and activist, LeBron is a legend on and off the court. As the records continue to tumble, here is his life and career in his own words.

Chapter 1

High School, High Hopes

Poor, at times homeless, and with only his mother standing between him and a life of crime, LeBron's guardian angels were hard at work clearing a pathway for him...

> **"**
>
> # My mother is my everything. Always has been. Always will be. **"**

On his mother Gloria's unwavering support and love throughout his life, notablebiographies.com.

The Facts #1

LeBron Raymone James Sr. was born in Akron, Ohio, on December 30, 1984. He was raised by his mother Gloria who was 16 when she gave birth, and his father Anthony McClelland played no part in his son's life.

Where I grew up – I grew up on the north side of Akron, lived in the projects. So those scared and lonely nights – that's every night. You hear a lot of police sirens, you hear a lot of gunfire. Things that you don't want your kids to hear growing up. When you're there and you know your mother's not home, you never know if those police sirens are for her.

Or if those gunshots were intended towards her. So those are the nights, almost every night, that would stand up hearing those sounds and hoping and wishing that it wasn't your parent on the other end.

"

On sleepless nights waiting for his mother to return from work, *Larry King Live*, June 2010.

I played for the Summit Lake Hornets, where I grew up playing basketball in 8-10 league. I was nine years old, and we won the championship. I was one of the best players on the team back then, so it was pretty fun.

On his first time on a basketball court, *Larry King Live*, June 2010.

The Facts #2

With no father figure and often no home of their own, LeBron and his mother would have to spend time staying with friends and relatives in Akron's projects.

Two men turned out to have influential roles when LeBron was aged nine – football coaches Bruce Kelker and Frank Walker, both gave a home to the Jameses to ensure they had stability and LeBron attended school regularly.

My life changed. I had shelter and food. I'll never forget what the Walkers did for me, especially Frank. He doesn't get the recognition he deserves because he's real quiet, but he was the first one to give me a basketball and the first one to show a real interest.

On how his temporary foster family helped change his life for the better, *The Guardian*, March 2003.

"

When did I know I had talent?
I think it started when I first started
playing sports, organized sports.
I played football for a team called
the East Dragons on the east
side of town. We only had six
regular season games. And six
games I played tail back and I had
18 touchdowns in six games.
That's when I knew I had some
athletic ability.

"

On first realizing he had athletic prowess, *Larry King Live*, June 2010.

High School, High Hopes

"

Michael Jordan was just my inspiration. I mean, the things that he was able to do out on the basketball court, I loved. Everybody wanted to fly like Jordan, pull up and hit a game winner at the sound of the horn like Michael. You wanted to do commercials, you wanted to have his shoes. You know, everything that he did, I wanted to do.

"

On following in his hero's footsteps, *Larry King Live*, June 2010.

66

As a kid, we would drive up and down 77 North – that's our highway – there would be office buildings on the side of the highway and I'd be like, that's what my house is going to look like when I get older. I'm going to start making my house look like this. Sometimes when I look at my house now and it's kind of bigger than some of those office buildings.

99

On dreaming of bigger and better things as a youngster, *Larry King Live,* June 2010.

The Facts #3

LeBron's basketball talents soon shone through, and as a teenager he was tipped by many to become a huge star.

Playing for the Catholic school he attended – St. Vincent-St. Mary High School – there was so much hype over LeBron that Time Warner even offered their games on pay-per-view!

You're not promised tomorrow.

A 17-year-old LeBron convinces his mother to let him play wide receiver for St. Vincent-St. Mary football team, arguing that nobody knows what tomorrow brings... *Sports Illustrated*, 2002.

The rule's not fair, but that's life. I'll stay another year because my friends are here. The only thing I think is bad, they let that 17-year-old golfer [Ty Tryon] on the PGA Tour. You've got tennis players competing professionally when they're 14. Why not basketball players?

On the NBA rule that prevents players being selected until their high school class graduates, *Sports Illustrated*, 2002.

"

Before anyone ever cared where I would play basketball, I was a kid from Northeast Ohio. It's where I walked. It's where I ran. It's where I cried. It's where I bled. It holds a special place in my heart. People there have seen me grow up. I sometimes feel like I'm their son. Their passion can be overwhelming. But it drives me. I want to give them hope when I can. I want to inspire them when I can.

"

On the love he has for his hometown, *Sports Illustrated*, 2014.

"

A lot of players know how to play the game, but they don't really know how to play the game, if you know what I mean. They can put the ball in the hoop, but I can see things before they even happen. A guy can make his teammates so much better. I learnt that from Jordan.

"

On being invited to a "bounce" game with Michael Jordan in Chicago when he was 16, *The Guardian*, March 2003.

"

Man, meeting Michael Jordan for me was like… black Jesus walking towards me. It was overwhelming to me to finally meet the guy I've looked up to my whole life.

"

On meeting his hero, *The Oprah Winfrey Show*, 2005.

My father wasn't around when I was a kid and I used to always say, 'Why me? Why don't I have a father? Why isn't he around? Why did he leave my mother?' But as I got older I looked deeper and thought, 'I don't know what my father was going through, but if he was around all the time, would I be who I am today?'

… It made me grow up fast.
It helped me be more responsible.
Maybe I wouldn't be sitting here
right now. 🙶

On growing up without his father and how
it shaped his life, *Sports Illustrated*, April 2012.

> **66**
>
> I was a sophomore in high school, and it was an unbelievable experience for me. It didn't even feel like he was on the face of the Earth. This guy was more like an angel, like an alien or something.
>
> **99**

On meeting his hero Michael Jordan for the first time, *Maxim*, October 2009.

❝

Being the only man in the
household with my mom definitely
helped me grow up fast.

❞

On his enforced maturity, *Men's Health*, 2010.

"

I believe the first All-Star Game that I actually sat down and watched was the – was it '97 in Cleveland? Because it actually came on local television, so we could watch it in Akron… '97. Kobe was a rookie. MJ was in that game. It was pretty cool for me and my friends. I think we were 11 years old at the time or 13.

"

On his earliest recollection of watching an NBA All-Star Game as a kid, NBA All-Star pregame press conference, Salt Lake City, 2023.

"

You have to be able to accept failure to get better.

"

On learning from his mistakes…

"

I like criticism. It makes you strong.

"

On taking positives from negatives...

"
I'm going to use all my tools, my
God-given ability, and make the
best life I can with it.
"

On his hunger to succeed and be the best...

All your life you are told the things you cannot do. All your life they will say you're not good enough or strong enough or talented enough. They will say you're the wrong height or the wrong weight or the wrong type to play this or be this or achieve this. They will tell you no.

A thousand times no. Until all the no's become meaningless. All your life they will tell you no. Quite firmly and very quickly. And you will tell them yes.

❞

Inspirational words from a man living in the projects who fought to become one of the wealthiest sportsmen on the planet...

The Facts #4

On June 26, 2003, LeBron was selected as Cleveland Cavaliers' first overall pick at the NBA draft at Madison Square Garden, New York.

I can handle it.

LeBron's response to reporters asking about the pressure and expectation that came with signing multi-million dollar sponsorship deals and endorsements after his first year with Cleveland Cavaliers – a statement he would make many times during his career, 2004.

> **"**
>
> I think team first. It allows me to succeed, it allows my team to succeed.
>
> **"**

On being a team player first and foremost…

"

You can't be afraid to fail. It's the only way you succeed – you're not gonna succeed all the time, and I know that.

"

On accepting there will be dips along with the highs, sportskeeda.com, November 2022.

Cleveland fans are awesome, but I mean, even my family gets spoiled at times watching me doing things that I do, on and off the court. **99**

On sharing his talent far and wide! *GQ*, August 2010.

"

I think the reason why I am who I am today is because I went through those tough times when I was younger.

"

On how his childhood troubles moulded him into the man he became…

Chapter 2

The Rise and Rise of LeBron James

From the moment he signed with the Cleveland Cavaliers, it was clear that LeBron was destined for greatness…

To all the positions, I just bring the determination to win. Me being an unselfish player, I think that can carry on to my teammates. When you have one of the best players on the court being unselfish, I think that transfers to the other players.

On his own ability, strength, and team play – LeBron was never short of confidence, even at the start of his career, Pre-Draft Press Conference, 2003.

I was just so, so nervous with excitement. Nervous with, I don't want to fail. I don't want to let people down.

"

On his first NBA points for the Cleveland Cavaliers against the Sacramento Kings in 2003, espn.com, January 17, 2003.

The Rise and Rise of LeBron James

"

I knew that I was ready for the moment. I knew that I belonged in the greatest league in the world. But I didn't know what to expect. And I was just super nervous. I didn't know how my first bucket was going to come.

"

On his NBA debut for Cleveland Cavaliers against Sacramento Kings in 2003, espn.com, January 17, 2003.

"

I don't want to be a cocky rookie coming in trying to lead right off the bat… If there's one message I want to get to my teammates it's that I'll be there for them, do whatever they think I need to do.

"

LeBron sets his stall out from the very start of his NBA career, notablebiographies.com, 2003.

The Facts #5

To have any chance of being a great basketball player, LeBron decided he needed as much rest as possible, with 12 hours per night a regular pattern for the teenager.

66

Thank God I didn't have social media; that's all I can say.

99

On his absence from social media at the start of his NBA career, where he believes he would have had to field all kinds of abuse and bullying, *The New York Times*, February 2023.

I watch Jordan more than anybody, for sure. But I'll watch tapes of AI too. I don't take anything from AI. Well, I do – his will. They say he was six feet, but AI was like 5'10.5". Do we even want to say 160? 170? Do we even want to give him that much weight? And he played like a 6'8" 2-guard.

He was one of the greatest finishers we've ever seen. You could never question his heart. Ever. He gave it his all. AI was like my second favourite player growing up, after MJ.

99

On the understated influence of Allen Iverson, *Maxim*, October 2013.

Pound-for-pound, probably the greatest player who ever played. He reminds me of Floyd Mayweather. You could never question his heart, his will to want to win. A true warrior.

More praise for Allen Iverson, *Maxim*, October 2013.

"

I always say, decisions I make, I live with them. There are always ways you can correct them or ways you can do them better. At the end of the day, I live with them.

"

On being decisive, for better or worse...

The Facts #6

LeBron became the first Black man to be featured on the cover of Vogue in April 2008. The only other men to appear on the cover prior to LeBron were Richard Gere and George Clooney.

"

Me being a big guy and a big supporter of fashion, to be on the cover with Gisele, on the cover of the biggest fashion magazine ever – it's pretty good.

"

On his *Vogue* cover shoot with Gisele Bündchen, espn.com, March 2008.

66

A LeBron James team is never desperate.

99

On whether the Cleveland Cavaliers were in poor form heading into the Eastern Conference semi-finals against Boston Celtics – Cavaliers would lose the game, 2008.

"

Yeah, 'ni hao'. [Hello.] That's the only one I need.

"

On his limited vocabulary in Mandarin following the 2008 Olympic Games in Beijing, *esquire.com*, September 2009.

It's real important in the sense of representing my country. I've done it the last two Olympics and it's been an unbelievable journey for myself to represent the national team.

On winning a gold medal for the USA at the 2008 Olympic Games, *The Guardian*, November 2011.

"

Absolutely. You know, sometimes he doesn't even know, but I told him on an Olympic team that I – in high school, when I was in high school and growing up, I had pictures of Kobe Bryant all on my walls, because he was like – you know, Kobe Bryant went straight to the NBA, so he was my inspiration. I was like wow!

"

On following in Kobe Bryant's footsteps, *Larry King Live*, June 2010.

I'm a winner… I'm a competitor. That's what I do. It doesn't make sense for me to go over and shake somebody's hand.

On receiving criticism following Game 6 of the 2009 Eastern Conference Finals for not shaking hands with the Magic.

66

If I could clone myself, we'd be all right.

99

On the upcoming 2009 Eastern Conference semi-finals against the Orlando Magic – and how a team of LeBrons would triumph!

Rest in Peace. I look up to and respect the likes of Joe Frazier and Muhammad Ali a lot. What I'm going through, and what professional athletes go through, is nothing compared to what someone like Ali went through – refusing to go to the army and facing prison.

Think of Bill Russell and what he went through as one of the first black basketball players on a professional team. Think of Jesse Owens… It was totally different. 99

On Joe Frazier's death and his place as a pioneer in the pantheon of iconic Black sportsmen and women, *The Guardian*, November 2011.

Jesse (Owens) and Joe (Louis), and Bill Russell and Muhammad Ali, paved the way for me. They paved the way for Magic and Jordan and Kobe and some of the greats in my sport. But we can go to other sports. Tiger Woods.

These guys… these great sports guys, these athletes, we play different sports, but we all live in the same house.

99

On his Black sporting inspirations – and housemates! *The Guardian*, November 2011.

Chapter 3

Just Puttin' It Out There

LeBron's decision to join the Miami
Heat in 2010 caused uproar in
Cleveland, and the outspoken LeBron
bit back – as well as venting his
spleen and occasionally reminding the
world of how good he was!

66

Hello World, the Real King James is in the Building. 'Finally'.

99

LeBron's first tweet, July 2010.

"

Don't think for one min that
I haven't been taking mental notes
of everyone taking shots at me this
summer. And I mean everyone!
"

On being criticized for The Decision,
bleacherreport.com, June 2011.

66

The last day I wanted it to be about me.

99

On why he didn't inform Cleveland Cavaliers he was joining the Miami Heat, bleacherreport.com, June 2011.

66

Warren Buffett told me once
and he always said follow your gut.
When you have that gut feeling,
you have to go with it, don't go
back on it.

99

On not being afraid to swim against the tide.

"

People will hate you, rate you, shake you, and break you.
But how strong you stand is what makes you.

"

On his character, conviction, and brushing off external opinions.

66

This fall, and this was a very tough decision for me, but this fall I will be taking my talents to South Beach and joining the Miami Heat.

99

On the infamous and controversial decision to join the Miami Heat in 2010…

66

If there was an opportunity for me to return, and those fans welcome me back, that would be a great story.

99

On the possibility of one day returning to the Cleveland Cavaliers, so soon after leaving them, *GQ*, August 2010.

66

Because it's LeBron's shoe. It is, it's got my name on it.

99

On his Nike shoes being higher priced than Kobe Bryant's, bleacherreport.com, June 2011.

"

There was like a 'F*** LBJ' T-shirt.
I believe they probably sold it at the
F***ing team shop. The Celtics had
something to do with that s***.

"

On feeling that the abuse he receives from Boston
is aligned between the team and fans, boston.com,
September 2022.

"

I still hate Boston. Don't get that twisted. We all hate Boston here.

"

On disliking the Boston Celtics and their followers, boston.com, September 2022.

66

Cause they racist as f***.

99

On Boston Celtic fans, boston.com,
September 2022.

"

Crazy. Karma is a b****. Gets you every time. It's not good to wish bad on anybody. God sees everything.

"

On the hostility he recieved from Cleveland Cavalier fans on his first return facing his old team, following the Cavaliers' 112-57 loss to LA Lakers, January 2011.

All the people that were rooting on me to fail, at the end of the day, they have to wake up tomorrow and have the same life that they had before they woke up today. They have the same personal problems they had today. I'm going to continue to live the way I want to live and continue to do the things that I want to do with me and my family and be happy with that.

They can get a few days or a few months or whatever the case may be on being happy about not only myself, but the Miami Heat not accomplishing their goal. But they have to get back to the real world at some point.

"

On his vocal critics wanting wishing for him to fail after the Miami Heat were beaten in the NBA Finals, 2012.

66

The Greater Man upstairs know when it's my time. Right now isn't the time.

99

On the Game 6 defeat to Dallas Mavericks as the Miami Heat's dream of winning the NBA Championship ends with a 4-2 loss, June 2011.

"

I lost touch with who I was as a basketball player and a person. I got caught up in everything that was going on around me, and I felt like I had to prove something to people, and I don't know why. Everything was tight, stressed.

"

On losing sight of what really matters, *Sports Illustrated*, April 2022.

Just Puttin' It Out There

"

This is what you love to do, and you've been doing it at a high level for a long time, and you don't really need to change anything. Just get back to what you do and how you play, smiling all the time and trying to dominate at the highest level. Do it with joy and do it with fun and remember that not too long ago this was a dream for you. Playing in the NBA was the dream.

"

On giving himself a reality check after losing to Dallas Mavericks at the 2011 NBA Championships during his time with the Miami Heat, *Sports Illustrated*, April 2012.

The Facts #7

Since the start of his basketball career, LeBron has accumulated numerous achievements in basketball, including:

4x NBA champion *(2012, 2013, 2016, 2020)*

4× NBA Finals MVP *(2012, 2013, 2016, 2020)*

4× NBA Most Valuable Player *(2009, 2010, 2012, 2013)*

19x NBA All-Star games *(2005–2023)*

3× NBA All-Star Game MVP *(2006, 2008, 2018)*

NBA Rookie of the Year *(2004)*

2x Olympic gold medallist Team USA *(2008, 2012)*

❝

It stayed with me a couple of months. It was definitely heart-breaking for myself, for my team, for our franchise and for the city. You just try and use those moments to be better next time… I really believe it's already made me a better player. And I'm a better person as well for it.

❞

On missing out on the NBA Championship after losing to Dallas, *The Guardian*, November 2011.

66

It definitely had a different feel, but it was a great moment for our team. I think that was a big step for our team, coming together. They all rallied around me because they knew what I was going through. We won that game and after that I think we won 23 out of 24 games. And I played OK too.

99

On returning to former team Cleveland for the first time, *The Guardian,* November 2011.

"

We had a rage. We weren't always perfect, but we played with rage, and we practiced with rage.

"

On his second season with the Miami Heat and using the disappointment of the defeat to Dallas Mavericks in 2011 as drive to win the 2012 NBA Championship, *Sports Illustrated*, November 2015.

"

Some of 'em, they boo you because they don't like you personally – but they don't know you personally… If they did, they might have a totally different idea about you. But some of 'em boo you because they care about their team. All they want is to see their team be victorious and I understand that.

"

On getting jeered by opposition fans – particularly on his visits back to Cleveland with Miami Heat, *The Guardian*, November 2011.

That came from the simple fact of how passionate and loyal those fans are. So that was a big part of it. But to walk through the facility the day before the game – to see all the history and all the achievements was very powerful. Liverpool have won 18 league championships, and it also meant a lot to read about King Kenny [Dalglish] and the story of Steven Gerrard – a hometown kid who now captains the team.

And then to just be at Anfield and see those 40,000 plus fans, screaming at the top of their lungs, the whole game, for 90 minutes, was an unbelievable experience for me.

"

On visiting Liverpool FC's Anfield and taking in a game, *The Guardian*, November 2011.

You know, it's just nice to be part of the team, to know the players and the history and what's going on with the team. Like I said, I'm humbled. I'm blessed. And I'm just excited about the future with Liverpool and the team – even right now you can feel they're building slowly towards becoming a league champion again.

On his minority stake in Liverpool FC, *The Guardian*, November 2011.

I believe that I was put here for a higher cause. We have people, not only today but over the course of time, that have been in the higher positions that chose to do it and chose not to do it.

On feeling responsible and using his voice to make a change, *GQ*, October 17, 2017.

> I don't think it's right or wrong. If it's in you, and if it's authentic, then do it. If it's some fake shit, then the people, the kids, they're going to notice it. They know.

On being genuine and believing in the causes he represents, *GQ*, October 17, 2017.

I say no because of always having to be on someone else's time. From the outside looking in, it seems like the president always has to be there – gotta be there. You really don't have much 'me time.' I enjoy my 'me time.'

On being asked whether he would like to be the President of the USA one day, *GQ*, October 17, 2017.

"

Your word has command to it.
If you're speaking with a
knowledgeable, caring, loving,
passionate voice, then you can
give the people of America and
all over the world hope.

On using his fame and popularity to help
and inspire others, *GQ*, October 17, 2017.

"

My state definitely voted for
Donald Trump, the state that
I grew up in. And I think I can sit
here and say that I have a lot of
fans in that state, too.
It's unfortunate.

"

On the heartland of many of his fans – the state
of Ohio – also being home to many ardent
Donald Trump supporters, *GQ*, October 17, 2017.

"

We live in two Americas and that was a prime example of that yesterday. If you don't understand or see that then you need to take a step back. Not just one step but four or five or even 10 steps backward. How do you want your kids or grandkids to live in this beautiful country? Because yesterday was not it.

"

On disliking Donald Trump and his supporters after they stormed Capitol Hill, *Sports Illustrated*, May 2022.

There is a comfort and a shadow and a protection here… This city protects me and my family. I can't explain it, but when I was a kid and I'd walk the streets or be out late or play on outdoor courts, I felt like people were watching me and thinking, 'Let's protect him'. I could feel that. I still feel it.

On returning to Cleveland and his fondness for the city, *Sports Illustrated*, November 2015.

Chapter 4

Family, Friends, and Heroes

A committed family man, proud father, and loyal husband who cherishes his friends and draws inspiration from his heroes. All those who LeBron brought with him on the path to legendary status.

"

Savannah was down when I was at my high school, no cameras, no lights. And she was there with me. You wouldn't be talking to me right now if it weren't for her.

"

On his wife and their shared history dating back more than 20 years, thehollywoodreporter.com, 2018.

The Facts #8

LeBron married his high school sweetheart Savannah Brinson in 2013. She was a cheerleader for a rival school of his when they started dating – they have three children together – sons Bronny and Bryce and daughter Zhuri.

Family, Friends, and Heroes

I ask him what are his aspirations,
and he says he wants to play in the
NBA. So, if he wants to do to it,
he's got to put in the work.
I'm here already, so, I'm just
waiting on him.

On son Bronny's potential move from college
basketball to the NBA, espn.com,
January 17, 2003.

"

He's already got some offers from colleges. It's pretty crazy. It should be a violation. You shouldn't be recruiting 10-year-old kids.

"

On son Bronny being approached at a tender age, *CBS Detroit*, 2015.

66

I'll foul the shit out of him! I'd give him all six fouls. I'd foul the shit out of Bronny, man.

99

On the possibility of playing against his son, Bronn, *GQ*, October 17, 2017.

"

I put it in the air because I like to talk to the basketball gods out there and see if things can come to fruition. I've always set out goals in my career, talked to the basketball gods, and they've listened to all of them. Hopefully, they can listen to this last one, too.

"

On extending his career so he can play alongside Bronny, *Sports Illustrated*.

My last year will be played with my son. Wherever Bronny is at, that's where I'll be. I would do whatever it takes to play with my son for one year. It's not about the money at that point.

On one last hurrah alongside Bronny, theathletic.com, February 2022.

Last night was such a surreal feeling for me. Watching my son play in our home state vs my Alma mater St. VM who's still being coached by my mentor, father figure, guy who coached and helped guide me throughout my childhood both on and off the floor Coach Dru Joyce II.

LeBron Instagram post after Bronny's winning points secure victory for Sierra Canyon School versus St. Vincent-St. Mary in the 2019 Scholastic Play By Play Classic.

Family, Friends, and Heroes

"

Video games is his thing.

"

On Bronny's favourite pastime, *Jimmy Kimmel Live*, 2021.

"

I want to thank the countless people sending my family love and prayers. We feel you and I'm so grateful. Everyone doing great. We have our family together, safe, and healthy, and we feel your love. Will have more to say when we're ready but I wanted to tell everyone how much your support has meant to all of us! #JamesGang👑

"

On the outpouring of support after son Bronny's cardiac arrest, Twitter, July 2023.

Still bittersweet, honestly. That's one of my best friends when I got into this league, even before I got into this league. We had so many moments when we were in high school, from competing against each other to sitting outside of a hotel room at 2 or 3 o'clock in the morning on the steps of a hotel and just talking about our journey up until where we were 17, I was 16, he was 17, and what we could possibly do going forward, what we could possibly do for our mothers, what we could possibly do for our families if we just continued to stay focused. I believe we was a driving force for one another. We were locked at the hip since high school.

"

On his close friend Carmelo Anthony announcing his retirement from basketball, asapsports.com, May 2023.

❝

Oh, like I've been saying over the last week, it was Kobe's last game before the break was in Cleveland. It was just bittersweet being out on the floor with him, knowing the matches between us two are coming to an end soon.

❞

On his in-game antics when facing Kobe Bryant for (almost) the last time on court, NBA All-Star Weekend press conference, February 2016.

"

There's a lot of things that die in this world, but legends never die.

"

On the first anniversary of Kobe Bryant's death, skysports.com, January 2021.

66

Man, there's a saying that says time heals all. As devastating and as tragic as it was and still is to all of us involved with it… it takes time. Everyone has their own grieving process.

99

On the first anniversary of Kobe Bryant's death, skysports.com, January 2021.

"

I have people around me, for the most part, that've been around me for a long time. So when you've been around people for a long time, there's no sugarcoating, there's no trying to put you higher than what you should be, there's no yes-men or -women, there's no gas. It's just straight-up, raw, uncut, unfiltered knowledge, truth, passion.

"

On having the perfect group of people around him to give him the best advice when he needs it, *GQ*, October 2017.

Commitment is a big part of what I am and what I believe. How committed are you to winning? How committed are you to being a good friend? To being trustworthy? To being successful? How committed are you to being a good father, a good teammate, a good role model? There's that moment every morning when you look in the mirror: Are you committed, or are you not?

On commitment being the most important tool for success.

"

The fact that I've been able to do what I love to do, play this sport and be able to transcend the youth… And being able to turn 30 and still doing it. I guess it means I've done some pretty good things to this point.

"

On his success being a product of spreading good in life, bleacherreport.com, 2014.

A person like myself always needs a great sidekick and a person you can rely on no matter the circumstances. And she's that. She's got my back and I love her for that.

On his talented daughter Zhuri,
Harper's Bazaar, 2010.

She needs no introduction to the world but I'm excited for you all to meet my Princess Zhuri Nova through her eyes. All Things Zhuri coming soon! Subscribe!!! #JamesGang👑

On his daughter's YouTube channel launch – aged 5! Twitter, December 2019.

121

Family, Friends, and Heroes

You know, my family and friends have never been yes-men: 'Yes, you're doing the right thing, you're always right.' No, they tell me when I'm wrong, and that's why I've been able to stay who I am and stay humble.

On keeping it real with those he trusts most, inc.com.

"

I always hoped that I could be able to put myself in a postion where I can give back, not only to to the youth, but to my own family. And to be almost 30 and to see my three kids and to see them grow, and for me to just try to give them the blueprint every day on what life is about and how to conduct yourself, that's the most important thing for me.

"

On using his success to give back to his family and act as a role model, bleacherreport.com, 2014.

"

He transcended sports and used his platform to empower people, which paved the way for all athletes and people of every race and gender that came after him, myself included.

"

On Muhammed Ali and his part in a HBO feature-length documentary, thehollywoodreporter.com, December 2016.

"

When I was a kid, I was amazed by what Ali did in the ring. As I got older and started to read about him and watch things about him, I started to realize what he did in the ring was secondary to what he meant outside of the ring – just his influence, what he stood for.

"

On Muhammed Ali's passing, June 2016.

"

I'm a pretty funny guy, and I would love to do a comedy with a bunch of funny guys – movie-star guys, where they could help me through it.

"

On a possible career after basketball, esquire.com, September 2009.

"

I don't want to say it ever becomes too much, but there are times when I wish I could do normal things. Like, walk into a movie theatre and sit down and go to the concession stand and get popcorn. I wish I could just go to an amusement park just like regular people. I wish I could go to Target sometimes and walk into Starbucks and have my name on the cup just like regular people.

"

On craving periods of normality, *The New York Times*, February 2023.

66

I need music. It's like my heartbeat, so to speak. It keeps me going no matter what's going on – bad games, press, whatever!

99

On his welcome distraction and lifeblood…

66

No way I would ever just stick to sports because I understand how powerful this platform and my voice is.

99

On making a difference with his success, medium.com, 2023.

Chapter 5

The History Boy

Akron's finest on achieving greatness...

The History Boy

"

It's motivating. It's great.
To know that everyone is trying to
build their team or wanting to get
their team to try to get to where
you are and try to knock you off,
it's a motivating factor. It's also
a humbling factor to know
that I've been in this position
for so long.

"

On being the player others look up to – and want
to knock off his perch! NBA All-Star Weekend press
conference, February 2017.

"

Nothing is given.
Everything is earned.

"

On working for a successful life.

I mean, I know how to put the ball in the hole.

On suggesting that he is not a natural scorer while approaching the all-time point record held by Kareem Abdul-Jabbar of 38,397, espn.com, January 17, 2003.

"

Breaking records or setting records or passing greats in a losing effort has never been a DNA of mine.

"

On the empty feeling of reaching personal NBA milestones when his team is losing, espn.com, January 17, 2003.

"

To be able to go out and still be a focal point of my opponent's scouting reports lets me know I'm still playing at a high level.

"

On keeping his standards as high as possible as time moves on, espn.com, January 17, 2023.

"

There's only three people in this world that can score on me in the post: Shaquille O'Neal in his prime – who else was it? Oh, it's two. And Jesus Christ.

"

LeBron – tongue firmly in cheek – on the "players" he would fear most, *Maxim*, June 2017.

66

I wanted to be Rookie of the Year,
I wanted to be an MVP in this
league, I wanted to win Championships, be an All-Star. I never said
I wanted to lead the league in
scoring, or for sure be the all-time
leader in scoring… To sit here
and actually be on the brink of
it actually happening is
pretty crazy.

99

On the surrealness of passing Kareem Abdul-Jabbar's
all-time NBA point-scoring record against Oklahoma
City, rolling stone.com, February 2023.

"

I've heard it's good for the heart. Listen, I'm playing the best basketball of my life, and I'm drinking some wine pretty much every day.

"

On his penchant for a glass or two of good red wine, *ESPN Magazine*, 2018.

Yeah, it made me want wine more! But I feel great. I feel great. I did a two-week cleanse and gave up a lot of things for 14 days.

On his 2018 pre-season diet regime while with the Lakers during which he abstained from wine, *The New York Times,* February 2023.

For me it's just a mindset. Training the mind. You train the mind, the body will fall where it may and take care of the rest.

On his fitness, stamina, and ability to play full games when needed at the age of 38, asapsports.com, May 2023.

> **"**
> I really don't. It's not who I am.
> I guess I'll reflect on my career when
> I'm done. But I don't know. I'll let
> you guys talk about it.
> **"**

On reflecting on Year 20 of his long career,
asapports.com, May 2023.

"

I love to play the game. I love to compete. I love to be out there for my guys, my teammates, whoever I have that particular year...

"

On how long he will continue to play and what keeps him going, asapports.com, May 2023.

The Facts #9

In 2004, LeBron created the LeBron James Family Foundation (LJFF) in his hometown, Akron, Ohio. What initially started as a mission to raise the graudation rates developed into a movement aimed to redefine family and community, with a focus on education and co-cirricular educational activities.

The I PROMISE program, a branch of the lJFF, has already provided 1400 students with resources for a better education.

66

Hopefully I made an impact
enough, so people appreciate what
I did, and still appreciate what I did
off the floor as well, even when I'm
done. But I don't live for that.
I live for my family, for my friends
and my community that needs
that voice.

99

On leaving a legacy, *The New York Times*,
February 2023.

> **"**
>
> I don't really think about it. I'm not a guy who kind of, like, basks in his accomplishments. I've won the championship four times in my career, and pretty much after the three parades or the celebration that we had, I was right back trying to figure out what the team was going to look like next year and how I can be better the following year. That's just who I am. **"**

On reaching NBA milestone after milestone, 2023 NBA Pregame Press Conference, Salt Lake City, February 19, 2023.

It's very challenging for all teams, not just us. It's something I've never experienced before in my career, and it doesn't allow you to – practice makes perfect, and it's true, but we have not had a lot of time to do that.

On playing during the COVID pandemic and adapting to the stringent restrictions in order to practice and play, Team LeBron press conference, March 7, 2021.

66

When you have that respect from
your teammates, it makes it a lot
more comfortable.

99

On having a good relationship with teammates.

"

I don't know how tall I am or how much I weigh. Because I don't want anybody to know my identity. I'm like a superhero. Call me Basketball Man.

"

LeBron on Marvel's next comic creation?

The History Boy

> **"**
> I thank you guys so much for allowing me to be a part of something I've always dreamed about. I would never in a million years dream this to be even better than what it is tonight.
> **"**

On surpassing Kareem Abdul-Jabbar's record 38,387 points total in 160 fewer games – just 10.9 seconds from the end of the third quarter in the Lakers' defeat to Oklahoma City Thunder, *The Mirror*, February 2023.

"

I am going to let everybody else decide who that is or just talk about it – but it is great barber shop talk.

"

On being regarded as the GOAT (Greatest of All Time) – and keeping barber shop talk interesting, *The Mirror*, February 2023.

66

I am going to take myself against anybody that has played this game, but everyone is going to have their favourite.

99

On the GOAT debate and being the record NBA points scorer, *The Mirror*, February 2023.

"

I feel like I could play for quite a while. So it's all up to my body, but more importantly, my mind. **"**

On continuing to play basketball, *Sports Illustrated,* August 2022.

> **66**
> If my mind can stay sharp and fresh and motivated, then the sky's not even a limit for me. I can go beyond that. But we shall see.
> **99**

On staying around for a few more years with the NBA, *Sports Illustrated*, August 2022.

66

After the Draymond (Green) finger to the eye, I was literally seeing three rims out there. So I just shot at the middle one.

99

On a dramatic 103-100 win over Golden State Warriors, talksport.com, September 2023.

The Facts #10

The LeBron James Family Foundation has raised and distributed more than $100 million to at least seven foundations, supporting at least 12 causes that grant four-year scholarships to students in his hometown.

This also included the $20 million LeBron pledged to building the I PROMISE school in Akron, Ohio, dedicated to serving the needs of underpriveledged and at-risk children.

66

LeBron stays humble just by being LeBron.

99

LeBron takes to talking in the third person on his humility...

Chapter 6

Let's Talk About LeBron...

Others have their say on LeBron James.

It's the points you score off the court that I am most proud of. You are empowering our kids and families in Akron and communities everywhere to reach their dreams.

Gloria James

LeBron's mother congratulates her son for his acheivements both on and off the court, 2023.

What LeBron has done off the court is more important than what he's done on the court. He's keeping kids in school. He's provided leadership and an exxample on how to live.

Kareem Abdul-Jabbar

The former NBA record holder's praise for "The King", *USA Today*, 2023.

Let's Talk About LeBron...

"

He's an outstanding talent. His greatest asset is he brings everyone else into the game. He makes his teammates look and play better. If you're pushing me – I'd say he's one of the 10 best of all time. Possibly.

"

Eddie Oliver

Editor of the Hoops USA website on LeBron's promise and teamwork, *The Guardian*, March 2003.

"

I started telling LeBron about passing the ball, how great players make their teammates better. I talked about getting his shots in the flow of the game. That was the last time I ever had to talk about LeBron shooting too much. "

Dru Joyce II

Summer league coach of St. Vincent-St. Mary boys basketball team and one of LeBron's first major influencers recounts the advice he gave to the-then 11-year-old.

Let's Talk About LeBron...

LeBron is a basketball genius, there is no other way to say it.

Keith Dambrot

LeBron's high school coach of two years on his star student.

"

We played Kobe when Kobe was a senior, and LeBron is the best player we've ever played against. LeBron is physically stronger than Kobe was as a senior, and we've never had anybody shoot better against us.

"

Jim Fenerty
The Germantown Academy coach after watching LeBron pile up 38 points and 17 rebounds in a 70-64 defeat of his Patriots in 2001.

You can only call it court sense.
The way he takes advantage of a
situation right away can't be taught.
He just has it.

Carlos Boozer

The Cleveland power forward reflects on Rookie of
the Year LeBron's first season with the Cavaliers.

66

LeBron has earned it. He's worked hard for 20 years. More power to him.

99

Kareen Abdul-Jabbar

The icon salutes the new NBA record points scorer after seeing his 34-year record finally surpassed by LeBron, *The Jennifer Hudson Show*, February 2023.

Let's Talk About LeBron...

I haven't put LeBron past Kobe Bryant yet. He's won a couple of rings, and now everybody is trying to compare him to Michael, who won six. What happened to Kobe? Kobe's still got five. LeBron has to win three more championships before he's in the Kobe Bryant class.

Charles Barkley

The NBA legend expresses what he feels LeBron needs to do to reach Kobe Bryant's level – and possibly Michael Jordan further down the line.

"

He setting the bar for what an athlete wants to be. Not everybody could do this. This is like the greatest that you could get. You see having that clear example for that now... He's set the precedent for basketball players for a long time.

"

Kevin Durrant

The Brooklyn Nets star discussing LeBron approaching the all-time record for most NBA points scored.

Let's Talk About LeBron...

L, congrats on being the all-time leading scorer in NBA history. It's even funny to just say that, you know coming from where you come from, how hard you grinded for this long. It's been an inspiration since day one. Much love and keep setting the bar high.

Kevin Durrant

More praise from Brooklyn Nets star, *The Mirror*, February 2023.

>> Wow, never in my lifetime did I think I would see two NBA athletes score over 38,000 points! I still remember when my Showtime teammate, the legendary Kareem Abdul-Jabbar, broke the record. It was an honor to be the guy to pass it to him and cement his legacy! <<

Magic Johnson

Joining the queue of legends lavishing praise on LeBron for becoming NBA's greatest points scorer, *The Mirror*, February 2023.

Let's Talk About LeBron...

Congrats @KingJames... legendary stuff right there. #38388.

Steph Curry

The NBA point guard reacts to LeBron's milestone moment. The number 38388 refers to LeBron's record-breaking score, *The Mirror,* February 2023.

66 True Greatness. Incredibly grateful to have witnessed and been a part of your journey. History made. 99

Kevin Love

Former Cleveland Cavaliers teammate congratulates LeBron on his points record, *The Mirror*, February 2023.

Let's Talk About LeBron...

20 years later, we are who we've always been – Witnesses to @KingJames' never-ending greatness. #WitnessGreatness

Nike tweet on their official account in praise of LeBron's new NBA points record, Twitter, February 2023.

"

It was also nice to just see him celebrate the roster, once we completed it, you know, a series of Instagram posts and different things, celebrating his teammates. And that's just the leader LeBron is. He knows how to galvanize a group and bring them together and we're just excited that he's behind that.

"

Rob Pelinka

LA Lakers general manager is grateful for LeBron's backing of his new recruits.

Let's Talk About LeBron...

I had three or four really good conversations with LeBron, about basketball, about life, about the importance of being a role model to younger kids. I was so impressed with his level of maturity. I kept saying to myself, 'This is a high school kid. This is a high school kid.' He was so mature, so focused.

Charlie Titus

The UMass Boston Hall of Famer on early meetings with LeBron. *Boston Globe.com*, July 2017.

"

Congratulations to LeBron on this incredible achievement. It's a testament to his hard work, longevity, and his great skill.

"

Michael Jordan

LeBron's hero praises him as he surpasses Kareem Abdul-Jabbar's NBA points record, *The Mirror*, February 2023.

He's a heck of a basketball player without a doubt.

Michael Jordan

A GOAT praising another GOAT.

"

I'm from Ohio, so I was aware of him pretty early. I saw him when he was a sophomore. His athleticism just then was amazing, but his basketball IQ was even better. Then I saw him again after that year and he was at a different level, after his sophomore year. He never plateaued. Still hasn't.

"

Brandon Hunter

The Boston Celtics forward on LeBron's never-ending talent.

Let's Talk About LeBron...

"

When I played in my first All-Star Game in Philly [during the 2001–02 season] there was a lot of people saying, 'This kid LeBron is so good, he could be in this All-Star Game right now.' I was like, 'What?' Man, Antoine [Walker] was always talking about him, telling me he could be better than all of us right then. **"**

Paul Pierce

The Boston Celtics forward on first hearing the (sobering) hype over LeBron.

"

At this time I was out of the country, and I hadn't been following high school hoops. I wasn't up on who LeBron James really was or what he was all about. So I started doing some research and I was like, 'There is no way this kid is 18 years old. That's the body of a grown man.'

"

Jerod Ward

The former NBA star on first seeing LeBron play.

I just thought he'd be a hometown hero for his era, and it would be over.

Savannah James

LeBron's wife and high school sweetheart never imagined how bright her future husband's star would shine.

"

I think the player that would fit with me the most, I actually think would be LeBron. He's a passer first, I'm a scorer, I'm a finisher. 'Bron is a facilitator by nature and I'm a finisher by nature. Those two styles, I think complement each other extremely well.

"

Kobe Bryant

The basketball legend on the player he'd have most wanted to play alongside in his prime.

Let's Talk About LeBron...

Welcome, brother. Welcome to
the family.

Kobe Bryant
A text sent by Kobe when LeBron joined the Lakers.

When he walks into a room he demands respect. And you listen to him. There's something about him.

Pat Riley

The Miami Heat President and NBA legend on LeBron's star quality, *The Guardian,* November 2011.

People look at stats, right? His stats are definitely going to be up there. To have passed Kareem Abdul-Jabbar, I can truthfully say that I'm jealous of that feat.

Shaquille O'Neal

Fellow player O'Neal on LeBron's NBA points record, *Sports Illustrated*, February 2023.

I think Ali would be very supportive of him because Ali went through the same thing in the past. He would really look up to James.

Khalilah Ali

The former wife of the legendary Muhammad Ali from '67 to '76, and mother of 4 kids with the boxing legend praises LeBron.

Let's Talk About LeBron...

Congratulations. I can remember coming to see you play in high school, 18 years old. I know what type of person you are, I know what type of player you are. 🙲

Shaquille O'Neal

On LeBron surpassing Kareem Abdul-Jabbar's points record.

"
I want to hear you say it!
Say it, Bron! Say it with your chest!
Say it, Bron!
"

Shaquille O'Neal

Urging LeBron to claim the title of the GOAT
on live TV.

Let's Talk About LeBron...

Understanding who LeBron is, and who he's been his entire career. The accolades and the championships he's won, and the records he has. He's an amazing basketball player and brings the best out of you. You know you have to be your best if you're gonna try to beat him.

Steph Curry

Praising his old adversary.

The Chosen One.

Jerod Ward

The former NBA star on first seeing LeBron play.

66

Check My Stats.

99

The words on a T-shirt sometimes worn by LeBron…